EDGE
BOOKS™

INFECTED!

INFLUENZA
HOW THE FLU CHANGED HISTORY

by Barbara Krasner

Consultant

James Higgins, PhD
Historian of Medicine

CAPSTONE PRESS
a capstone imprint

Edge Books are published by Capstone Press,
1710 Roe Crest Drive, North Mankato, Minnesota 56003
www.mycapstone.com

Library of Congress Cataloging-in-Publication Data
Names: Krasner, Barbara, author.
Title: Influenza : how the flu changed history / by Barbara Krasner.
Description: North Mankato, Minnesota : Capstone Press, [2019] | Series:
  Infected! | "Edge Books are published by Capstone Press." | Audience: Ages
  8-14. | Audience: Grades 4 to 6. | Includes bibliographical references and
  index.
Identifiers: LCCN 2018036906 (print) | LCCN 2018038213 (ebook) | ISBN
  9781543555097 (ebook) | ISBN 9781543555004 (hardcover : alk. paper)
Subjects: LCSH: Influenza Epidemic, 1918-1919--Juvenile literature. |
  Influenza--History--20th century--Juvenile literature. |
  Influenza--Prevention--Juvenile literature. | Diseases and
  history--Juvenile literature.
Classification: LCC RC150.4 (ebook) | LCC RC150.4 .K73 2019 (print) | DDC
  616.2/03--dc23
LC record available at https://lccn.loc.gov/2018036906

Editorial Credits
Editor: Maddie Spalding
Designer: Craig Hinton
Production Specialist: Ryan Gale

Quote Sources
p. 6, Richard Rubin, *The Last of the Doughboys.* Boston: Houghton Mifflin Harcourt, 2013; p. 12, "The Great Pandemic of 1918: State by State." *Flu.gov,* n.d.

Photo Credits
Alamy: Gado Images, 17; AP Images: Marco Ugarte, cover (people); CDC: C. S. Goldsmith and A. Balish, 8, Emily Cramer, 28–29; Library of Congress: American National Red Cross Photograph Collection, 10, Marion S. Trikosko/U.S. News & World Report Magazine Photograph Collection, 22; Newscom: BSIP, 15, Everett Collection, 19, Liu Tao/FeatureChina 26–27, Raj Wong/FeatureChina, 20–21; Shutterstock Images: Everett Historical, 5, 11, 12, GPPets, 18, Jamie Wilson, 7, Sebastian Kaulitzki, cover (virus); The National Guard: Sgt. Darron Salzer, 24–25

Design Elements
Shutterstock Images: ilolab

TABLE OF CONTENTS

CHAPTER 1

SICK AT SEA

On September 29, 1918, 19-year-old Reuben Law boarded a ship in New York. The ship was bound for France. Law was a soldier in the U.S. Army. The United States had joined World War I (1914–1918) in 1917. Law and many other soldiers were headed to France to fight against Germany and its allies.

Two days into his journey, Law wrote in his diary that he felt very sick. He was in a state of confusion called **delirium**. Delirium is a **symptom** of influenza. Law had the Spanish Influenza, or the Spanish flu. This type of flu infected millions of people worldwide in 1918.

delirium—a state of confusion that may be a sign of a disease, such as influenza
symptom—a change in a person's body or mind that is a sign of a disease

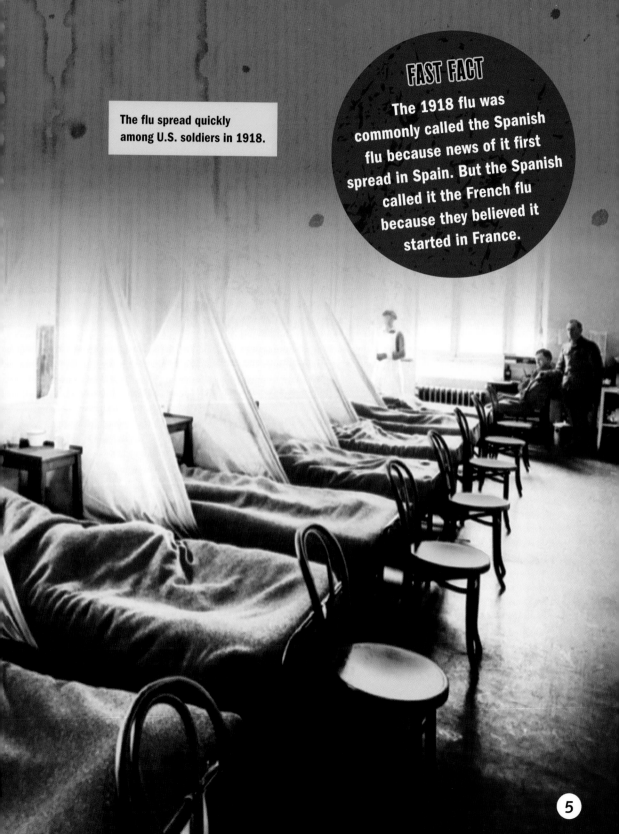

The flu spread quickly among U.S. soldiers in 1918.

FAST FACT

The 1918 flu was commonly called the Spanish flu because news of it first spread in Spain. But the Spanish called it the French flu because they believed it started in France.

FLU OUTBREAKS

The 1918 Spanish flu was not the first deadly flu outbreak. The first known widespread flu outbreak occurred in 1510. It started in Africa and spread to Europe. In 1580 another flu spread. It began in Asia. Then it spread to Africa, Europe, and North America. It became a global outbreak in just six weeks. In 1889 a flu outbreak began in Russia. It spread quickly throughout Europe. It then affected North America, South America, and Asia. About 1 million people died from the Russian flu.

Law was not the only soldier on the ship to come down with the flu. Many others did too. Soon the ship's dining room had to be converted into a hospital. Law and other ill passengers were packed together. Law remembered, "They put two tables together and there'd be two of us, and I, my head was next to the feet of the guy next to me. . . . We had little pads, but that didn't amount to much." For about one week, Law cycled through periods of fever and delirium. The bodies of men who died from the flu were tossed out to sea. By the time the ship arrived in France in October 1918, 91 soldiers had died from the flu. But Law was fortunate. He survived.

FLU SYMPTOMS

The flu is a **virus**. It is **transmitted** when an infected person coughs or sneezes. A healthy person breathes in the virus. The virus multiplies inside a person's body. It attacks the nose, throat, and lungs.

There are many different flu symptoms. The illness can come on suddenly with chills, fever, and headaches. **Mucus** builds up in a person's lungs. This leads to coughing and muscle pain. In the most severe cases, people experience delirium.

A fever is a common symptom in the early stages of the flu.

virus—something that causes disease by reproducing and growing inside a person's body
transmit—to pass on something from one living thing to another
mucus—a thick liquid that is produced in the nose and throat

FLU TYPES

There are four types of influenza viruses. They are called A, B, C, and D. Influenza C viruses usually cause mild illness. Influenza D viruses tend to infect only cattle. These viruses have never infected people. Influenza A and B types are the seasonal flu. In the United States, the seasonal flu appears every fall and winter.

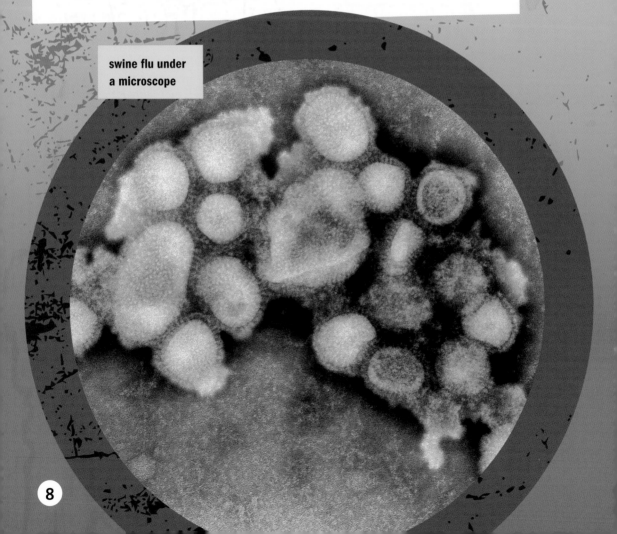

swine flu under a microscope

Influenza A has subtypes based on combinations of two different proteins. These proteins are found in the virus. They are called hemagglutinin (H) and neuraminidase (N). Different subtypes are called strains. There are more than 100 different strains of influenza A based on different H and N combinations. The most well-known example of a dangerous flu strain is H1N1. This strain caused the Spanish flu.

FAST FACT

Birds or pigs can spread the H1N1 virus to humans. Scientists are not sure which type of animal spread the 1918 Spanish flu to humans.

Influenza viruses are first carried in the guts of wild birds. Some of these viruses can be transmitted directly from birds to humans. This type of influenza is called the bird flu.

Some flu strains are passed from birds to pigs. This type of influenza is called the swine flu. The virus then can pass from pigs to humans.

THE SPANISH FLU

Most historians today think the Spanish flu started in Asia. Because the flu spread around the world in 1918, it was called a **pandemic**. It reached the United States in the spring of 1918. It spread among 50,000 soldiers at Camp Funston, an army camp in Kansas. The soldiers did not develop symptoms right away. They did not know that they carried the virus.

Volunteers for the American Red Cross prepare stretchers to carry flu victims in 1918.

pandemic—an outbreak of a disease that spreads across several countries or continents and affects many people

Infected soldiers traveled to other parts of the United States. They spread the flu to other people. Some people died just hours after they first developed symptoms. The virus quickly spread throughout big cities such as Philadelphia and New York. It also spread to smaller communities.

Ships carrying soldiers or goods to other countries also carried the flu virus. Soon the flu had spread to many places around the world, including Europe, Africa, and South America.

FAST FACT

Ohio's Camp Sherman had more deaths from the flu than any other U.S. military camp. Nearly 1,200 soldiers at Camp Sherman died in 1918.

Doctors and nurses tried to treat soldiers who came down with the flu.

Some soldiers rinsed their mouths with salt and water, a method they thought would help get rid of the flu.

FIGHTING THE FLU

People in 1918 did not know the exact cause of the flu. But they did understand that flu germs were spread through the air. Some families sealed up their homes. Flu survivor Lee Reay lived in Utah at the time. He remembered that one family "closed up every possible avenue of letting fresh air into the house. . . . They plugged up keyholes on the door, sealed windows, and stayed inside, breathing their own air."

Communities came up with some ways to fight the flu. Public spaces such as schools were closed. It became illegal in many places for people to gather in crowds. These measures did reduce the number of flu cases. But the flu still spread quickly.

Doctors could treat the symptoms of the flu. They used a new medicine called aspirin. Aspirin helped to reduce fever, swelling, and pain. But it did not cure people of the flu. Between September 1918 and March 1919, the Spanish flu killed about 50 million people. This was about 3 percent of the world's population. Overall one-third of the globe fell ill.

FLU MASKS

Between 1918 and 1919 public health officials gave flu masks to millions of people in the United States. They ordered people to wear these masks. They hoped the masks would keep people from getting the flu. The masks were worn over the mouth and nose. People who didn't wear masks were forced to pay a fine. They also were not allowed to take public transportation. But the masks did not work very well. They were made from thin fabric, such as cotton or linen. The virus could still pass through spaces in the masks. Today's flu masks are more effective. They are made of thicker fabric that does not allow viruses to pass through.

CHAPTER 3

STUDYING THE FLU

In 1918 most scientists thought the flu was caused by a **bacterium**. German doctor Richard Pfeiffer had studied flu patients during a pandemic in 1892. He had found bacteria in the patients. He believed the bacteria had caused the flu. Scientists created **vaccines** from the bacteria. But the vaccines did not work very well. Scientists would not discover the true cause of the disease until the 1930s. More scientists began to study the disease after a number of flu outbreaks occurred in the early 1900s.

bacterium—a small organism that lives in water, in soil, or in the bodies of plants and animals
vaccine—a substance made up of dead, weakened, or living organisms that is injected into a person to protect against a disease

In September 1918 the National Swine Show and Exposition opened in Cedar Rapids, Iowa. Large crowds of people gathered at the show. Within days some of the pigs became ill. They came down with fevers. They coughed and sneezed.

After the show closed in October, people brought the pigs back to their farms. Infected pigs began to spread the virus to other pigs throughout the Midwest. Thousands of pigs died. People discovered that these pigs had died from the swine flu.

Scientists today continue to study the H1N1 flu virus that killed millions of people in 1918.

Another outbreak of the swine flu happened in Iowa in 1928. Scientist Richard Shope began to investigate this illness. Shope had grown up on a farm in Iowa. He was familiar with swine diseases. He had read scientific papers that discussed a link between the swine flu and the Spanish flu.

Shope and another scientist named Paul Lewis experimented on pigs. They wanted to find the cause of the swine flu. Shope believed that something in the mucus of the pigs had spread the flu. He collected mucus from infected pigs. He filtered the mucus. He injected healthy pigs with it. The healthy pigs became sick. Filtering the mucus had removed bacteria. So Shope knew that bacteria had not caused the flu. A virus was left behind. Shope's method proved that a virus caused the flu.

Pfeiffer's bacillus under a microscope

FAST FACT

An accident in a laboratory proved that animals could pass the flu to humans. A sick ferret sneezed in a researcher's face. The researcher came down with the flu.

Meanwhile researchers in England experimented with ferrets. They injected ferrets with **blood serum** from people who had survived the Spanish flu. The animals became ill. This proved that animals could get the flu from humans.

After the true cause of the flu was discovered, scientists did more experiments to develop a vaccine. Researcher Thomas Francis experimented with flu viruses in the 1930s. He gave a dose of a flu virus to mice and ferrets. He let the animals heal from the illness. Then he gave them a dose of a different flu virus. They did not get the flu the second time. Their bodies had developed ways to fight the virus. They were **immune**.

blood serum—a yellowish fluid found in the blood that is useful for laboratory tests
immune—unaffected by something that causes a disease, such as a virus

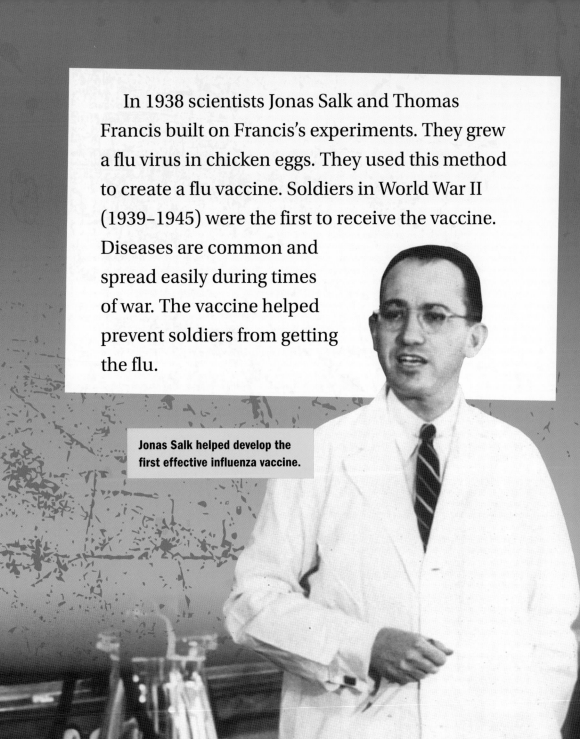

In 1938 scientists Jonas Salk and Thomas Francis built on Francis's experiments. They grew a flu virus in chicken eggs. They used this method to create a flu vaccine. Soldiers in World War II (1939–1945) were the first to receive the vaccine. Diseases are common and spread easily during times of war. The vaccine helped prevent soldiers from getting the flu.

Jonas Salk helped develop the first effective influenza vaccine.

CHAPTER **4**

VACCINATIONS

The flu vaccine helped prevent outbreaks of known flu viruses. But the influenza A virus has many strains. Researchers made this discovery in 1936. They found that the strains kept changing. These ever-changing strains made it hard for scientists to keep the vaccine up to date.

New influenza A strains caused outbreaks throughout the mid-1900s. A deadly outbreak of the H2N2 flu hit China in 1957. It quickly moved eastward. It killed about 3 million people within the span of five months. The H3N2 strain emerged in Hong Kong, China, in 1968. It spread to the United States when soldiers returned home after the Vietnam War (1954–1975). It killed more than 1 million people around the world.

Most flu vaccines today are grown in eggs.

Gerald Ford was the U.S. president during the swine flu scare of 1976.

FAST FACT

In 1976 celebrities were photographed receiving the flu vaccine. These photos helped promote the vaccine.

THE 1976 FLU SCARE

On February 4, 1976, 19-year-old David Lewis was stationed at an army base in New Jersey. He came down with a fever. He ached all over. He shivered and had a headache. A doctor told him to go to bed. But he joined his unit on a hike. He gasped for air and collapsed. He died a few hours later in the hospital.

Scientists gathered samples from Lewis's body to determine the cause of his death. The Centers for Disease Control and Prevention (CDC) identified the strain that had killed him as the swine flu. People were afraid there would be another flu pandemic. The U.S. government predicted the 1976 swine flu would kill 1 million Americans. U.S. president Gerald Ford began an **immunization** campaign in 1976 against the swine flu. More than 40 million Americans were vaccinated.

immunization—the process of using a vaccine to prevent infection

The disease did not spread as predicted. The virus infected only 13 people. Lewis was the only person to die from it. But one maker of the vaccine mixed up its viruses. The vaccine was made to treat a different strain of the flu. More than 500 people became partially **paralyzed** after receiving the vaccine, although doctors are unsure whether the vaccine was the cause. Twenty-three people also died. The government stopped the immunization program for the swine flu.

Scientists learned from the mistakes of the 1976 vaccine. The vaccine had been made from a living virus.

paralyzed—unable to move all or part of the body

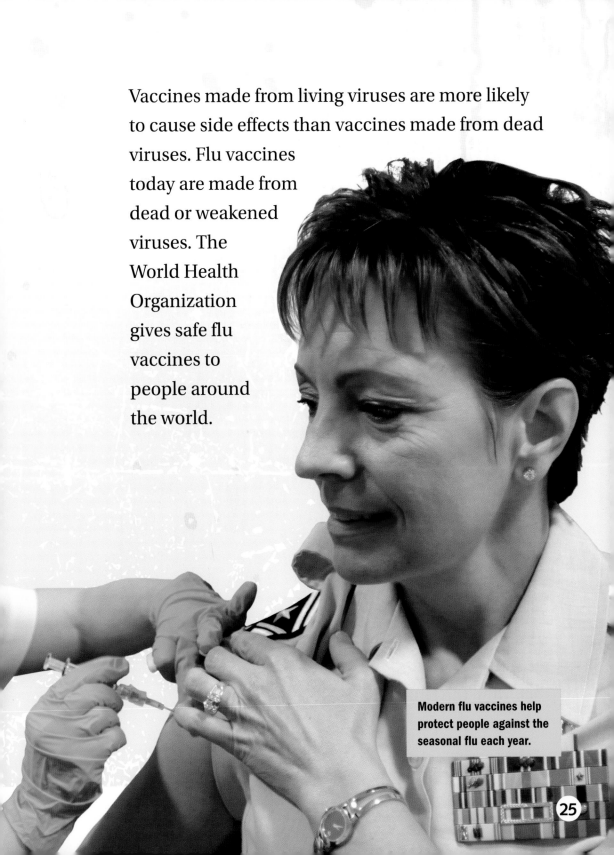

Vaccines made from living viruses are more likely to cause side effects than vaccines made from dead viruses. Flu vaccines today are made from dead or weakened viruses. The World Health Organization gives safe flu vaccines to people around the world.

Modern flu vaccines help protect people against the seasonal flu each year.

CHAPTER 5

THE THREAT CONTINUES

In the past, a flu pandemic occurred about once every 10 to 30 years. Flu vaccines have helped reduce the number of outbreaks. But global health experts expect a new flu strain to cause another pandemic at some time in the future. The most recent flu pandemic occurred in 2009. The H1N1 swine flu spread from Mexico to countries around the world, including the United States.

Two vaccines were required to fight the 2009 flu pandemic. The pandemic killed about 284,000 people worldwide.

A teacher in China checked children for flu symptoms during the 2009 swine flu pandemic.

Drug companies develop vaccines each year to protect people from the current flu strains. The CDC recommends that everyone six months and older get a flu vaccine each fall. But these flu shots can only protect against strains that are known. Flu shots are also not 100 percent effective. The CDC recommends steps that people can take to avoid getting or spreading the flu, such as cleaning objects that may carry germs.

Today most people who get the flu recover from it. Yearly immunizations can protect people against different flu strains. Companies have also developed drugs to treat flu symptoms. But scientists are still studying the 1918 virus to find out why it was so deadly. In 2010 scientists confirmed that the current H1N1 and H3N2 strains developed from the 1918 H1N1 strain.

FAST FACT

Each year between 5 and 20 percent of the U.S. population gets the flu.

Because new strains are always emerging, the flu will never be eliminated. But scientists today work to improve flu vaccines. Health officials will continue to develop ways to protect against flu viruses.

A scientist studies flu viruses at the Centers for Disease Control and Prevention.

GLOSSARY

bacterium (bak-TEER-ee-uhm)—a small organism that lives in water, in soil, or in the bodies of plants and animals

blood serum (BLUD SEER-uhm)—a yellowish fluid found in the blood that is useful for laboratory tests

delirium (di-LEER-ee-um)—a state of confusion that may be a sign of a disease, such as influenza

immune (i-MYOON)—unaffected by something that causes a disease, such as a virus

immunization (IM-yoo-ni-zay-shuhn)—the process of using a vaccine to protect against infection from disease

mucus (MYOO-kuhss)—a thick liquid that is produced in the nose and throat

pandemic (pan-DEH-mik)—an outbreak of a disease that spreads across several countries or continents and affects many people

paralyzed (PA-ruh-lized)—unable to move all or part of the body

symptom (SIM-tuhm)—a change in a person's body or mind that is a sign of a disease

transmit (TRANZ-mit)—to pass on something from one living thing to another

vaccine (vak-SEEN)—a substance made up of dead, weakened, or living organisms that is injected into a person to protect against a disease

virus (VY-ruhss)—something that causes disease by reproducing and growing inside a person's body

READ MORE

Henry, Claire. *The World's Deadliest Epidemics.* The World's Deadliest. New York: PowerKids Press, 2014.

Micklos, John. *The 1918 Flu Pandemic: Core Events of a Worldwide Outbreak.* What Went Wrong? North Mankato, Minn.: Capstone Press, 2015.

Peters, Marilee. *Patient Zero: Solving the Mysteries of Deadly Epidemics.* Toronto, Canada: Annick Press, 2014.

INTERNET SITES

Use FactHound to find Internet sites related to this book.

Visit www.facthound.com

Just type in 9781543555004 and go.

Check out projects, games and lots more at
www.capstonekids.com

INDEX